WATCH FOR THESE
ADDITIONAL BOOKS
WRITTEN BY

Susan Olson Higgins:

THE PUMPKIN BOOK

THE THANKSGIVING BOOK

THE ELVES' CHRISTMAS BOOK

THE BUNNY BOOK

THERE'S A GIGGLE IN MY POCKET

PUMPKIN PRESS

P.O. Box 139
Shasta, CA 96087

Written and illustrated by Susan Olson Higgins.

Pumpkin Press Publishing House
P.O. Box 139
Shasta, CA 96087

ISBN 0-939973-06-5

The Valentine Book

*Full of Cupid's
History, Poems, Songs,
Art Projects, Games,
Language Arts,
and Recipes*

Written and Illustrated by
Susan Olson Higgins

DEDICATED TO

PREFACE

Spread a little love ... everyday! Choose an assignment below
and share it with someone you know ... or don't know.

** Tell a friend you care.

** Say something nice to three people today.

** Help someone who feels rejected, lonely, or afraid.

** Tell your teacher or mother "Thank You" for
something nice that she did for you.

** Smile and wave at an old friend.

** Tell someone, "You can do it!"

** Wait for someone who is lagging behind and walk
with him.

** Feed your pet/s without being told.

** Clean up after yourself without being told.

** Give a hug to someone in your family.

And have a Happy Valentine's Day!

Susan Olson Higgins

This year . . .

Recycle!

Reuse

Create

Make your own Valentine's Cards

Originate

Decorate

. . . help save our Earth!

TABLE OF CONTENTS

THE STORY OF ST. VALENTINE

by Ray Van Diest

As the centuries have unfolded, it has become difficult to separate romantic invention from the actual facts in the true story of St. Valentine. But it is believed Valentinus (St. Valentine's Latin name) was a Christian in pagan Rome. He became known as a Saint for his brave and giving deeds. He helped and comforted Christian martyrs who were suffering from persecution under the Roman ruler, Emperor Claudius, who ruled from A.D. 268-270.

Claudius had forbidden his men to marry because they might think too much about home and family rather the shining armor and winning battles. He wanted dedicated soldiers to fight for the Roman Empire. But Valentinus ignored Claudius' decree and performed Christian weddings, which were illegal. When the Emperor discovered this, he was outraged. He had Valentinus, a good and kind man, thrown into prison for a year.

But Valentinus remained strong. During that year in prison, he continued steadfastly in his faith and his commitment to spread Christianity. He even converted his jailer, Asterius, and his family to Christianity. The jailer had a lovely daughter who was blind. Legend has it that Valentinus miraculously restored her sight.

Valentinus maintained his dignity and courage throughout his stay in prison. Claudius was impressed with Valentinus' strength and virtue. In fact, he tried to convert Valentinus to worship the Roman gods and idols. But of course Valentinus would do nothing of the kind. In an angry rage, he severely condemned Claudius' religion. In an act of revenge, Claudius sentenced Valentinus to be beaten with clubs and killed. Later, Valentinus was named a Saint for his sacrifices and Christian deeds.

It was only a few years after Valentinus' martyrdom that Christianity became the Roman state religion. The priests were anxious to do away with pagan tradition, so they renamed Roman festivals after Christian saints. One of these days was named St. Valentine's Day. So this is how the ancient Roman traditions became linked with our celebration today, and how this holiday became known as St. Valentine's Day.

1

VENUS AND CUPID

As the myth has been told through the ages ...

There once was a goddess so lovely that people worshipped her as the goddess of love and beauty. The Greeks called her Aphrodite, and the Romans called her Venus.

Aphrodite had a son whom the Greeks named Eros and the Romans named Cupido, or Amor. We call him Cupid. He had wings which allowed him to fly about. But he was a bit of a scamp. He enjoyed watching people suffer or profit in love.

He carried a bow and a quiver of arrows with him wherever he went. Some of his arrows were gold-tipped, while others were tipped with lead. When Cupid shot the gold-tipped arrows into people, they would fall in love, whether they wanted to or not! When Cupid shot the lead-tipped arrows, his victims would feel miserable, forlorn, unable to love whether they wanted to or not. No wonder Cupid's love was called 'bitter-sweet'!

Today, we don't often remember Cupid's bad side. Instead, we emphasize the romantic love between people. Our image of Cupid remains full of warm and happy thoughts of the little cherub or angle with wings.

VALENTINE CARDS

In the 17th century, Samuel Pepys (pronounced Peeps) recorded in his diary the giving of the very first Valentine card. On February 14, 1667, he wrote about a small boy who brought Mrs. Pepys a charming gift of her name written on a page of blue paper with elegant gold letters. Samuel Pepys and his wife were delighted with the enchanting idea! So, later that day at a Valentine's Day party, a new tradition began. The guests designed romantic mottoes and drew fancy letters for each person's name. And so the Valentine's Day card has evolved, now filled with artistry and verses for those we love and care about.

THE HISTORY OF MAIL DELIVERY

by Ray Van Diest

The history of the mail service dates back to over 4,000 years ago. Even back then, the delivery of mail depended a great deal on an extensive network of roads, way stations, and people to carry the mail from point to point. Often runners or riders have been used through history to carry the mail in the form of a relay race, passing it from one carrier to the next. The post office today is still based on this principle.

The Romans under Augustus Caesar organized the most intricate and successful of the ancient mail systems in the first century B.C. Augustus had impressive, well constructed road systems throughout the vast Roman Empire. Couriers mounted horses and raced between relay stations called 'posthouses.' In fact, that is where we get the name for our 'post offices' today!

In colonial America, it was very expensive to use the British Government's postal service. So, the citizens secretly set up their own routes and used private carriers. Benjamin Franklin improved the dependability and frequency of postal deliveries when he was an assistant Postmaster General for the colonies in the 1750's. When the Revolutionary War began, the Continental Congress named him its Postmaster General.

A century later, in 1860-61, the famous Pony Express rode through dangerous territory between St. Joseph, Missouri, to Sacramento, California. They made the one-way trip in a week and a half, racing station to station on horseback. But they were in business for only about two short years. The telegraph and the railroad system took over the transporting of mail, which put the Pony Express out of business.

In 1911, the first airmail was flown by plane from Garden City to Mineola, New York, by Earle Ovington. What a change from the early days of mail service! Within a decade, airplanes were carrying mail on regularly scheduled flights. Now, of course, we can send our Valentine cards and letters all over the world in just a few days!

A Heart Full of Poems

FEELIN' GOOD

by Susan Olson Higgins

Give a hug,
Squeeze a hand,
Nod your head,
Feelin' grand!

Snuggle up,
Pinch a chin,
Wink an eye,
Share that grin!

Snap your fingers,
Give 'em five,
Ain't it great
To be alive?

DONNA McDOOGAL McMAJORS McBAY

by Susan Olson Higgins

Donna McDoogal McMajors McBay
Said that she'd come to my house to play.

She entered the room through my dresser drawer.
She looked at the cat and asked, "Does it snore?"

She flew to the window, then back to the rug.
She flopped on a pillow and colored it "bug."

She nodded three times and turned into a toy.
She picked up the bed and made it a boy.

She took a bandana, a pretzel, and stew,
And turned them all into a cow that said, "Moo!"

She sprang to the ceiling, upside down.
She opened the door, and in stepped a clown!

Then sweetly she sang, "It is time to depart!"
She left through the closet in a chocolate heart!

Donna McDoogal McMajors McBay
Left giggles and fun for Valentine's Day!

If all the world would be polite,

There would never, ever be a fight.

. . . said Karen Poellet one sunny day.

6

FRIENDSHIP

by Susan Olson Higgins

Friendship . . .
    a giggle,
    a wink,
    we share what we think.

    Together
    or no,
    a warm, happy glow.

    Night
    or noon,
    it's never too soon.

    A gift
    that's true
    from me to you . . .
Friendship.

VALENTINE CHANTS

by Susan Olson Higgins

Alfalfa sprouts
Bumpy bridge
Put my heart
Up on your 'fridge.

    Sweet pickles
    Clothes lines
    Let's be
    Valentines!

Rain sprouts
Tattered hats
Be mine,
Just like that!

    Crunchy beets
    Old shoes
    This heart
    Is Just For You!

NOW YOU MAKE UP A VALENTINE CHANT!

THE VALENTINE BEAR

by Susan Olson Higgins

The sleepy old bear
At the bottom of the stair
Is waitin' for me to come.

He twists and snores
And stretches some more
Waitin' for Valentine fun.

He reaches his paws,
Extends his claws,
And tangles them in the rug.

His long shaggy coat
Makes him look like a goat,
That over-grown furry bug.

He tries and tries
To hide his size
But that's impossible to do.

I love that bear
At the bottom of the stair,
Oh, I'm sure that you would, too!

Yup! He's waitin' there
At the bottom of the stair
For Valentines' Day, you see.

It's hard to wait
For that playful date . . .
He's Awake!
   . . . and roarin' for me!

He grumbles and growls
He paces and prowls
Wondering when our games can start.

So together we go
Marchin' kinda' slow
While he licks a chocolate heart.

Then we fish and hike,
Chomp berries, fly kites,
Slide down waterfalls.

We hide and seek,
Hop Adam's Creek,
Chase rolling pinecone balls.

We toss and romp,
We skitter and stomp
Through field and grass and stream.

It's so much fun
To tumble and run.
We're a twosome! A Bear-y team.

I give him a hug
And a honey-lickin' jug,
'cause now it's time to part.

He gives me a smile
In V.-Bear style
That snuggles right into my heart.

Then he nestles there
At the bottom of the stair,
To snoozle the way Bears do.

And that sleepy old Bear,
He'll be waitin' there
For you - know - who!

(This one's for you,

Co-op Kids, with love!)

9

THE VALENTINE TREE

by Susan Olson Higgins

Come with me
To the Valentine Tree
Where you will find sweets and prizes.
You may collect
What e'er you select
From all the delightful surprises.

Fill your pockets
With chocolate lockets
Climb up the purple branches.
Nibble and munch
A heart-shaped lunch
Gather oodles of magic chances.

If we find the key,
Tucked in the tree
Then we will be asked to stay!
So follow me
To the Valentine Tree
Where joy and happiness play.

THE VALENTINE MAN

by Susan Olson Higgins

Swing, swing, whenever you can,
But don't swoop past the Valentine Man.

Swing, swing, on silver vine,
Reaching out for Valentines.

He molds the lacy Valentine shapes,
The rings, the lockets, the heart-shaped cakes.

The man will nod and say, "Hey, hey!
I'll share my hearts on Valentine's Day."

He'll give away those dainty hearts
He stores inside his fancy cart.

If you go to him on silver thread,
He'll give you slices of Valentine bread.

So tumble down and pick a few,
Pink and red, and gold, and blue.

Swing, swing, o'er daphodils,
Just beyond the Purple Hills.

Swing, swing, whenever you can,
But don't swoop past the Valentine Man!

11

THE PRICE IS LOVE!

by Susan Olson Higgins

Hearts for sale!
Hearts for sale!
Who will buy
These hearts for sale!

Some are open.
Some suppose.
Some are purple.
Some turn rose.

Some are crinkled.
Some can shrink!
Some run clock-wise.
Some will wink!

Just one rule
I must make,
Never, EVER
Let one break.

Treat them kindly.
Show them care.
These precious hearts
Are very rare.

Do not store them.
Hand them out!
Your friends will treasure
Them, no doubt.

Hearts for sale,
Hearts for sale,
Who will buy
These hearts for sale?

HOW MANY HEARTS?

by Susan Olson Higgins

One heart
Two hearts
Three hearts
Four . . .
    Twirl three times through
    the Old Wood Door.

Five hearts
Six hearts
Seven hearts
Eight . . .
    Skip right over
    to the Golden Gate.

Nine hearts
Ten hearts
Eleven hearts
Twelve . . .
    Hand-painted Cups
    on the Lace-Covered Shelves.

JESSICA'S DAY

by Susan Olson Higgins

Do you know what she got on Valentine's Day?
A little red locket, a basket of clay!
    Forty-two cards filled with verses and hearts,
    Five candy kisses and two Sweet Tarts.
Marshmallows, chocolates, and twenty-three flowers,
A brand new watch to watch the hours.
    One lacy doily all covered with red,
    A gros-grain ribbon to pretty her head.
And a telephone call from Aunt Linda and Phil,
And a little glass bird for her window sill.
    Some pretty new gloves, purplish-pink,
    And a teddy bear soap to sit by her sink.

But her FAVORITE part of Valentine's Day
Was a Hug!
    . . . and when her friends came to play.

13

FIVE LITTLE VALENTINES

(an action poem)

by Susan Olson Higgins

Five little Valentines
Playing in a tree,
The first one said,
"Oh, come, look at me!"
    (hold up dangling hearts)
The second one said,
"I can touch the sky!"
    (reach up high)
The third one said,
"Watch me fly!"
    (swoosh hand back and forth)
The forth one said,
"Feel the wind blow!"
    (blow on hearts)
The fifth one said,
"Swing high, swing low!"
    (swing hand high and low)

Then a red bird came
To the Valentines' tree
    (open and close thumb and pointer of other hand)
And said, "Valentines,
Fly away with me!"
    (Valentines fly away with bird.)

*(You may wish to dangle hearts
from their fingers, too!)*

VALENTINE TICKLES

by Susan Olson Higgins

Valentine, Valentine, sprinkle your giggles
Skip through the clouds made of bubbles and jiggles.

Hop over tulips, bounce over walls,
Valentine, listen, the raindrops calls.

Valentine, Valentine, slide through time.
Then, sweet Valentine, will you be mine?

WHERE'S YOUR HEART

(action poem)

by Susan Olson Higgins

*(Before you begin reading this
poem, draw a tiny heart on the
index finger of each child)*

Put your heart on your elbow,
Put your heart on your nose,
Put your heart on your stomach,
Put your heart on your toes.

Put your heart on your earlobe,
Put your heart on your thigh,
Put your heart on your knee cap,
Put your heart above your eye.

Put your heart on your waist,
Put your heart on your chest,
Put your heart somewhere new,
So your partner can guess!

*(Each child should touch a new spot
with the index finger. Another child
should name the spot!)*

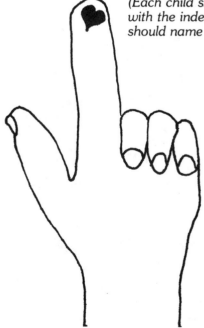

15

SLAP-CLAP-VALENTINE

(action poem)

by Susan Olson Higgins

(Set the beat before you begin.)
(Slap-clap
Slap-clap
Slap-clap
Slap-clap)

Slap your thigh
Clap your hands
We're going to make
A "rhythm band."
    (continue to slap-clap)

Slap and clap
To the beat
Stand right up
And stomp your feet!
    (stomp feet to the beat)

Slap and clap
Turn around
Catch that rhythm
Catch that sound!
    (pretend to catch the rhythm)

Slap and clap
Feelin' fine
You're going to
Be my Valentine!
    (point to your Valentine)

LET IT IN!

by Susan Olson Higgins

If I were
    I were
Made of tin

Then never
    Ever
    Ever
Could love
        Come in.

LETS PRETEND

(an action poem)

by Susan Olson Higgins

Grab a partner
Take his hand
Together make
A rubber band.
  ("stretch" in and out)

Twist and turn
Get all set
Now you make
The alphabet!
  (Make a,b,c, etc.)

You'll crawl down low
Sooner or later
If you become
An alligator!
  (pretend to be an alligator)

Make your eyes
Blink, blink, blink,
When you give
Mr. Moon a wink!
  *(hold arms above head for a
  moon, then wink at it)*

Hold on tight!
Don't let go!
Drive your car
V-e-r-y slow!
  (pretend to drive a car)

Bend and shape
Take a part
Two become
A Valentine heart!
  *(each child makes a heart
  with hands, arms or legs)*

17

THE POSTMAN

(an action poem)

by Susan Olson Higgins

*(As you read this poem, have the
children move in a circle to each verse.)*

The postman walks	The postman skips
Along the street	Along the street
Delivering mail	Delivering mail
Through sun	Through sun
And sleet.	And sleet.
Walk	Skip
Walk	Skip
Walk.	Skip.

The postman stomps	The postman runs
Along the street	Along the street
Delivering mail	Delivering mail
Through sun,	Through sun
And sleet.	And sleet.
Stomp	Run
Stomp	Run
Stomp.	Run.

(Make up verses of your own!)

"Neither snow, nor rain, nor heat, nor gloom
of night stays these couriers from the
swift completion of their appointed
rounds"

*Inscription on the N.Y. Post Office
adapted from Herodotus, Greek Historian,
Fifth Century B.C.*

SHAPE THE EARTH

by Susan Olson Higgins

Our earth is shaped
In a roundish sphere
But if I could,
I would change it here.

I would mold it new
To a giant heart
Everything on it
Would have a new start.

Everything on earth
Would learn to share
Love . . . pure love
Would permeate the air.

ALL mankind would
Treat each other
As if all tribes
Were sister and brother.

Sunshine showers
Would radiate a glow
Kindness and care
Would overflow.

Animals would trample
Every evil deed
They would travel far
To plant forgiveness seeds.

Keys to happiness
Hidden all around . . .
If you picked one up,
A giggle would sound.

Fish and brooks
Clouds and trees
Would shimmer with joy
In the friendship breeze.

Our earth IS shaped
In a roundish sphere
But if I could . . .
Yes, I would change it here.

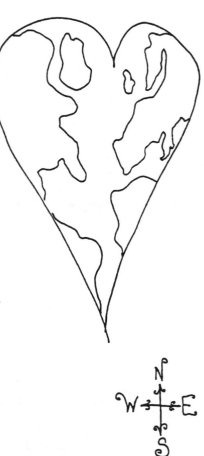

Oh,
Sing to Your
Heart's
Content!

TEACH THE BEAT WITH . . .

Listen To The Rhythm Of Your Heart Beat
(an action poem)

by Susan Olson Higgins

Listen to the rhythm
of your heart beat . . .
    lub dub
    lub dub
    lub dub   *Slow*

Step to the rhythm
of your heart beat . . .
    lub dub
    lub dub
    lub dub

Clap to the rhythm
of your heart beat . . .
    lub dub
    lub dub
    lub dub

Sway to the rhythm
of your heart beat . . .
    lub dub
    lub dub
    lub dub

Now sing to the rhythm
of your heart beat . . .
    lub dub
    lub dub
    lub dub

(Make up your own verses here!)

VALENTINE DANCE

(action poem)

by Susan Olson Higgins

BOOM cha, cha, cha,
BOOM cha, cha, cha,
BOOM um, pah, pah,
BOOM cha, cha, cha.

BE cha, cha, cha,
MY cha, cha, cha,
VAL um, pah, pah,
ENTINE cha, cha, cha.

BOOM cha, cha, cha,
BOOM cha, cha, cha,
BOOM um, pah, pah,
BOOM cha, cha, cha.

Note: Make up dance steps to go with the rhythm of this
rhyme.

THE TEENY, TINY VALENTINE

(tune: "Itsy Bitsy Spider")

by Susan Olson Higgins

The teeny, tiny valentine
Sat down among the trees,
Along came a spider
And sat upon his knee.
The teeny, tiny valentine
Hopped up and ran away.
Oh, he won't be back until
Valentine's Day.

The teeny, tiny valentine
Was strolling through the park,
Down went the sun
And up popped the dark.
The teeny, tiny valentine
Was tickled as could be,
While he watched evening stars
Twinkle through the trees.

The teeny, tiny valentine
Found a friendly horse.
"Would you like a ride?"
He said, "Yes, of course!"
So the teeny, tiny valentine
Climbed up on top.
He wished and wished and wished
His ride would never stop!

(Can you make up more
adventures for the teeny, tiny
valentine?)

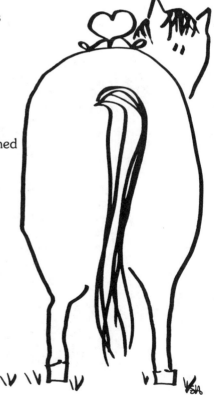

COLOR OF MY HEART

(tune: "Farmer in the Dell")

by Susan Olson Higgins

The valentines are here
The valentines are here
Heigh-ho, de-doodle-o,
The valentines are here.

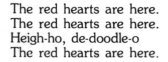

The blue hearts are here.
The blue hearts are here.
Heigh-ho, de-doodle-o,
The blue hearts are here.
   (The children wearing blue go to center.)

The red hearts are here.
The red hearts are here.
Heigh-ho, de-doodle-o
The red hearts are here.

   (The children wearing red go to the center.)

(Continue singing until all children have been included.)

Note: *You might wish to distribute different colored hearts for the
children to hold up as the verses are sung. Later, they can
switch colors to practice recognition. If you have no colored
hearts, identify colors of clothes they are wearing! For older
children, write words or numbers on the hearts to substitute for
colors and make up verses to sing those words.*

CATCH THE SUN

(tune: "Row, Row, Row Your Boat")
by Susan Olson Higgins

Run, run, Valentine,
In the circle, please,
Run, run, catch the sun,
Then chase after me.

Skip, skip Valentine
In the circle, please,
Skip, skip, catch the sun,
Then chase after me.

Prance, prance, Valentine,
In the circle, please,
Prance, prance, catch the sun,
Then chase after me.

Gallop, gallop, Valentine,
In the circle, please,
Gallop, gallop, catch the sun,
Then chase after me.

OR:

Run, run, Valentine,
In the circle, please,
Run, run, catch the sun,
Then chase after me.

Skip, skip, Valentine,
In the circle, please,
Skip, skip, over the moon,
The chase after me.

Prance, prance, Valentine,
In the circle, please,
Prance, prance, over the hill,
Then chase after me.

Gallop, gallop, Valentine,
In the circle, please,
Gallop, gallop, through the waves
Then chase after me.

Walk, walk, Valentine,
In the circle, please,
Walk, walk, through the leaves,
Then chase after me.

25

ROYAL ASSISTANCE

by *Susan Olson Higgins*
(tune: "I'm A Little Teapot")

I'm the royal cobbler
As you can see
I tap, tap, hammer, hammer
Merrily
   (tap, tap, hammer your palm)

I will make a valentine
For you from me.
   (point to a friend, then to self)

I'll cut and stitch the leather
Carefully.
   (pretend to cut and stitch)

I am the royal seamstress
As you can see
I cut, pin, and sew like a
Busy bee,
   (pretend to cut, pin, sew and stitch)

I will stitch a valentine
For you from me,
I will cut, cut, clip, snip
Happily.

I am the royal carpenter
As you can see
I saw and hammer
Perfectly.

I will build a valentine
For you from me
I will saw, saw, tap, tap,
One, two, three.

   (Divide the class into groups of cobblers, seamstresses, and carpenters. Have the groups take turns singing their parts.)

Art
from the

Heart

JOSHUA'S SPLATTERED VALENTINE

MATERIALS YOU WILL NEED

one pre-cut 6"x6" heart
red, blue, purple, yellow tempera paint
paint container
paint brush
newspaper
magic marker

WHAT TO DO

1. Cover an area with newspaper.
2. Place the heart on the paper.
3. Carefully tap the wet brush on your finger over the heart so the paint splatters on the heart.
4. Splatter different colors on the heart.
5. Set aside to dry.
6. Using a magic marker, write a message on the heart.

VALENTINE GARDEN STICK

MATERIALS YOU WILL NEED

pre-cut 3"x3"x1/4" wooden valentine
   from a craft shop
1/2" dowel rod
wood glue
acrylic paints
water color paint brushes
toothpicks
newspaper
water to clean brushes
small collection of seeds

WHAT TO DO

1. Glue the dowel rod to the heart.
2. Set aside to dry.
3. Lay out newspapers.
4. Paint the heart with the acrylic paints, using the paint brushes and toothpicks to add details to the heart.
5. Set aside to dry.
6. Give it with a small collection of seeds as a Valentine gift!

VALENTINE FELT BIRD

MATERIALS YOU WILL NEED

4 to 10 pre-cut felt hearts
scissors
white or tacky glue

WHAT TO DO

1. Arrange the hearts in the shape of a bird.
2. Glue the hearts together
3. Set aside to dry.
4. Make up a poem or song to a tune you know about your bird.

VALENTINE BOUQUET

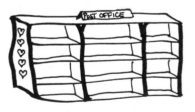

MATERIALS YOU WILL NEED

red crepe paper
florist tape and wire
scissors

WHAT TO DO

1. Cut the crepe paper into circles with a diameter of approximately 5-7".
2. Gently twist the center of the circle around the florist wire, leaving the edges open like "petals."
3. Wrap the base of the flower to the "stem" or wire with florist tape.
4. Gently stretch the paper at the edges to create a more natural look.
5. Make three to five flowers. Give them as a bouquet for Valentine's Day!

VALENTINE POST OFFICE

MATERIALS YOU WILL NEED

one shoe box per child
red tissue paper or
    other wrapping paper
scissors
glue
stapler
name tags

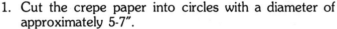

WHAT TO DO

1. Wrap each box inside and out with wrapping paper. Glue or staple the paper onto the box.
2. Stack all of the boxes in rows on top of each other to make post office mail boxes. Secure them with staples or glue.
3. Place name tags in each mail box.
4. Deliver Valentine mail to this post office on Valentine's Day!

PETER'S VALENTINE BOOKMARK

MATERIALS YOU WILL NEED

one 2"x5" felt piece
one 2"x2" felt pre-cut heart
tacky glue

WHAT TO DO

1. Glue the felt heart on the top of the 2"x5" felt piece to make a bookmark.
2. Set aside to dry.
3. Give the Valentine bookmark in place of a Valentine card!

CARVE A SOAP HEART

MATERIALS YOU WILL NEED

butter knife
tooth pick
one bar of hand soap
an adult to supervise

WHAT TO DO

1. Be SURE to discuss safety when using a knife. This activity is **not appropriate for very young children.**
2. Carve an outline of the heart on the soap with the tip of the tooth pick.
3. Carve the soap heart by whittling only small shavings at a time.
4. Be sure to whittle **away** from your hand!

HUG-A-DOLL

MATERIALS YOU WILL NEED

two pieces of material pre-cut in the
   shape of a person
florist wire or bread ties
tacky glue
felt tip pens

WHAT TO DO

1. Draw a face, hair and other details on the doll using felt tip pens.
2. Lay the wire in the center of the doll on the wrong side of one of the pieces of material.
3. Glue it in place.
4. Spread glue over the wrong side of the second piece of material. Match and place the wrong sides together to complete the doll.
5. Set it aside to dry.
6. Bend arms and legs to make the doll twist and turn.
7. Make one, two, or more dolls. Bend their arms any which way!

WHAT'S INSIDE A HEART?

MATERIALS YOU WILL NEED

crayons
pre-cut 12"x12" heart shape
tape of quiet, classical music

WHAT TO DO

1. Discuss some of the loving feelings we have, how we affect others, and how we respond to love.
2. Put on a quiet tape of classical music. Listen to it while drawing a picture of sharing love. Allow creativity and expression.
3. Make a list of vocabulary words the children used to describe their art from the heart.

THE VALENTINE TREE

MATERIALS YOU WILL NEED

branch
small pail
sand or plaster of paris
spray paint
string
scissors
red construction paper

WHAT TO DO

1. Spray paint the branch white or red.
2. Place it in the pail and secure it with sand or plaster of paris.
3. Cut 3"x3" heart shapes out of the red construction paper.
4. Fold the hearts over and over, then cut them as you would a snowflake to make a lacy effect.
5. Hang the hearts on the tree with string.
6. For variety, add other Valentine art projects to the tree, such as your hug-a-doll, heart-shaped pillow, etc.

ANDREA'S VALENTINE MAGNET

MATERIALS YOU WILL NEED

3"x3" felt square
2½"x2½" felt square
   (both different colors)
scissors
glitter
small magnet
tacky glue

WHAT TO DO

1. Cut both felt squares into heart shapes, one larger than the other.
2. Glue the smaller heart to the center of the larger heart.
3. Write the word LOVE with glue on the small heart.
4. Set aside to dry.
5. Glue magnet on the back.
6. Set aside to dry.
7. Put it up somewhere with a Happy Note attached. ("Have a great day!", "Thanks!", "You are special!", "I love you!," etc.)

KEYS TO MY HEART

MATERIALS YOU WILL NEED

one 12"x8" pre-cut key
1"x 1" pre-cut red hearts
material scraps
gold or silver spray paint
rik-rak, glitter, etc.
scissors
tacky glue
string

WHAT TO DO

1. Spray paint the key. Set aside to dry.
2. Decorate the key with glitter, hearts, and material scraps.
3. Hang the key from a string with the Heart Pillow.

Variation: Place a variety of shapes of keys on paper and spray paint lightly over them to make a print of the keys. Title the piece, "KEYS TO MY HEART."

PEACE PARADE

MATERIALS YOU WILL NEED

large rolls of newsprint
tempera paints
brushes
water and containers
scissors

WHAT TO DO

1. Discuss the meaning of peace and how we can all contribute to it in our homes, on the playground, in school, and throughout the world. Explain that you are going to have a "Peace March."
2. Fold the paper in half and cut two large hearts at one time, leaving them connected at the top. Cut a small slit in the center top for the head to fit through.
3. Open and lay them flat. Paint the outside of each heart with designs and messages.
4. Set aside to dry.
5. Put them on. Have a peace parade.

STITCH A HEART PILLOW

MATERIALS YOU WILL NEED

needle
thread
5"x5" red material pre-cut in the shape
of a heart
scissors
polyester stuffing

WHAT TO DO

1. With right sides together, stitch 1/4" around from the edge of the red heart, leaving a 2-1/2" space unstitched along one edge to stuff it later.
2. Turn the heart right side out.
3. Stuff it with polyester filling or old nylon stockings.
4. Pull the open edges together and stitch the opening closed.
5. Stitch a small loop near the center top of the pillow so it can be hung on the wall or from the Valentine tree.

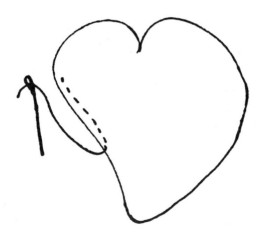

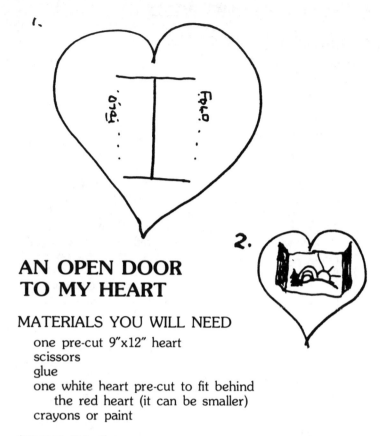

AN OPEN DOOR TO MY HEART

MATERIALS YOU WILL NEED

one pre-cut 9"x12" heart
scissors
glue
one white heart pre-cut to fit behind
  the red heart (it can be smaller)
crayons or paint

WHAT TO DO

1. Cut an "I" shape in the center of the red heart from top to bottom. Fold back the "doors" to open and close.
2. Draw or paint a design or scene which depicts "What is inside your heart?" on the white paper.
3. Glue the white paper onto the back of the red heart so that the picture will be visible when the doors of the red heart are opened.
4. Decorate the outside of the red heart.

DESIGNER DISH TOWELS

MATERIALS YOU WILL NEED

plain muslin white dish towels
material markers and pens
heart-shaped stencils

WHAT TO DO

1. Place the stencils along one edge of the dish towel. Draw the heart border using the stencil and material markers.
2. Lift the stencil and decorate the heart with different colors and designs.
3. Set it aside to dry.
4. Wrap it up and give it as a very special Valentine's Day gift!

Variation: Embroidery stitch on a pattern the child has drawn on the dish towel.

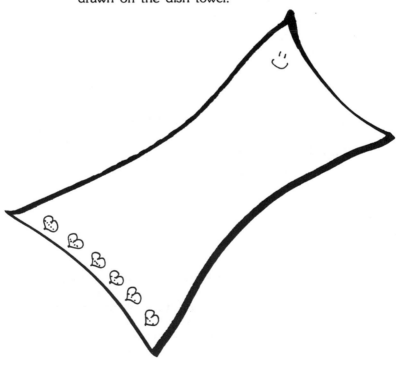

VALENTINE'S TREE ORNAMENTS

MATERIALS YOU WILL NEED

tin foil
material scraps and ribbons
pre-cut tag board or cardboard hearts
   (various sizes)
red tissue paper or material
white glue
string
hole puncher

WHAT TO DO

1. Decorate the pre-cut hearts by gluing the tin foil, material scraps, and ribbons on to them.
2. Use hole puncher to punch a hole in each heart near center top.
3. Cut different string lengths and attach to each heart.
4. Hang them on the Valentine's Tree where they can twirl and dance in the breeze.

MURAL FULL OF HEART

MATERIALS YOU WILL NEED

Valentine gift wrapping paper
magic markers or crayons
scissors
glue
6"x6" construction paper

WHAT TO DO

1. Pre-cut a huge heart from the Valentine gift wrapping paper.
2. Have the children illustrate the meaning of love and ways to share love on 6x6" construction paper.
3. Cut around each child's illustration and glue them inside the enormous Valentine gift wrapping paper heart.
3. Display it!

VALENTINE DANCING MAN

(He'll make you laugh whenever he moves!)

MATERIALS YOU WILL NEED

two 5"x5" construction paper squares
four 2½"x2½" pre-cut hearts
hole puncher
yarn
10-12" stick or twig
magic markers or crayons
dancing music

WHAT TO DO

1. Cut hearts from the construction paper squares.
2. Decorate a face on one of the 5"x5" hearts with magic markers or crayons.
3. Using the hole puncher, punch holes in the top and bottom of the two 5"x5" hearts. Now punch a hole in the top and bottom of two of the smaller hearts. Punch only one hole at the top of the last two smaller hearts, leaving the bottom without a hole.
4. With the yarn, connect the two larger hearts approximately 2" apart for the body of the puppet.
5. Now connect the hands and feet to the body with the yarn.
6. Connect the head and two hands to the stick to complete the puppet!
7. Now put on the music and let your Valentine man dance!

FRAGRANT VALENTINE CARD

MATERIALS YOU WILL NEED

one sheet 9"x12" construction paper
white glue
red jello powder
pencil

WHAT TO DO

1. Fold the paper in half to make the card.
2. Write a message on the inside.
3. On the cover, pencil in heart designs very lightly.
4. Glue over the pencil lines and where color should be added.
5. Sprinkle the jello powder over the wet glue. Allow it to dry flat.
6. It smells delicious!

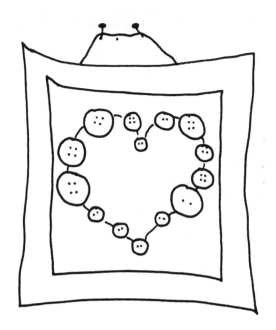

CATHY'S HEART-FULL
OF BUTTONS

MATERIALS YOU WILL NEED

about 12—14 small buttons
either tacky glue (for younger children)
OR needle and thread (for older children)
7"x7" inch heavy, non-printed fabric
a pre-cut construction paper frame and
    backing to go over the 7"x7" fabric
pencil

WHAT TO DO

1. Lightly sketch a large heart on the material square.
2. Glue OR sew the buttons onto the fabric in the heart shape.
3. Glue the fabric onto the back.
4. Glue the construction paper frame over the fabric square front.
5. Hang it on the wall to remind someone you love them!

HEART-PRINT STATIONERY

MATERIALS YOU WILL NEED

one pre-cut thick cardboard heart
  with a small cardboard handle
glued on
red, pink or blue tempera paint
newspaper
pie tin
5½"x8½" paper

WHAT TO DO

1. Lay the newspaper out on the table.
2. Pour just enough thick paint in the pie tin to cover the bottom.
3. Dip the cardboard heart in the paint. Let the excess drip off.
4. Press the heart on the stationery page where you want the design. Lift it carefully straight up so it does not smear.
5. Set aside to dry.
6. Make as many as you wish. Wrap and give them as a Valentine gift!

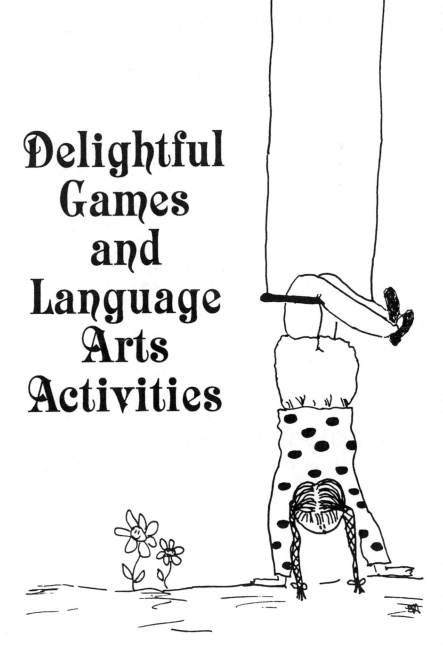

Delightful Games and Language Arts Activities

VALENTINE DETECTIVE

MATERIALS YOU WILL NEED

one 1/2"x1/2" red paper heart
masking tape

WHAT TO DO

1. Roll a tiny piece of masking tape and stick it to the back of the heart.

2. Have all of the children sit behind a designated line, except the child who is IT.

3. Have the child who is IT leave the room and hide the heart somewhere on his/her body. It can be under the shoe, on the elbow, behind the ear, anywhere!

4. Have IT return. The children waiting must guess where the heart is hiding. The child who guesses correctly is IT for the next game.

CUPID'S TARGET PRACTICE

MATERIALS YOU WILL NEED

one pre-painted bull's eye
three beanbags
masking tape

WHAT TO DO

1. Set up the bull's eye against a safe wall with masking tape.

2. Using the three bean bags, practice hitting the target.

3. Have competition to see who can score the highest points!

MATCHING HEARTS

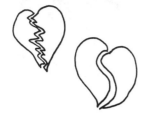

MATERIALS YOU WILL NEED

6x6" hearts cut in half like a puzzle
   so that only those halves match
     (one heart per child)
thumb tacks

WHAT TO DO

1. Tack one half of each heart to different trees and fence posts outside. Give the other matching half of the heart to a player.
2. The players then go outside and find the missing half to their heart and "mend the broken heart" by returning with the matching halves.
3. For younger children, hide hearts with matching colors rather than cutting the hearts in half.
4. This can also be done on a flannel board for younger players.

VALENTINE ON MY TOE

MATERIALS YOU WILL NEED

one 3"x3" Valentine bean bag
starting line
finishing line

WHAT TO DO

1. All players line up on the starting line.
2. Place a Valentine bean bag on each player's toe.
3. On "Go!" players race to the finish line, keeping the Valentine bean bag on the toe. If it falls off, player either returns to starting line to begin again, or places it back on the toe and continues from that spot.
4. The first player to the finish line is the winner.

Variation: For older children, place one Valentine bean bag on each foot at the same time, then race to the finish line.

49

A VALENTINE CONTEST

MATERIALS YOU WILL NEED

one 6"x6" pre-cut heart per child
pencil, magic markers or crayons
Word List
hat

WHAT TO DO

1. Give each student a heart and either a pencil, magic marker, or crayons to draw with.
2. Read the Word List.
3. Allow each child to choose one of the words from the Word List. (If you have young children, be sure to simplify this activity and read the words to them.) Do NOT allow other children to hear or read the word!
4. Have the children draw a face to illustrate their word.
5. Read the word list again. Ask each child to hold up his work while the rest of the class guesses which word matches the face. Be prepared for lots of fun!
6. Have the children write a story about their character, using their word from the Word List at least once. Young children can share a continuing tale, adding a portion about their Valentine face.
6. It might be fun to record these efforts on a cassette!

WORD LIST:

jovial
silly
happy
broadest grin
ridiculous
hilarious
smilingest
delightful
goofiest
funniest
preposterous
outrageous
feistiest
merriest

mirthful
gleeful
vivacious
cheery
light-hearted
happy-go-lucky
exuberant
blissful
ecstatic
congenial

HEART-PENNY DROP

MATERIALS YOU WILL NEED

one red pre-cut heart about the
size of this page
three pennies
tape
three small red paper hearts, a
bit larger than a penny
a sturdy chair or stool

WHAT TO DO

1. Tape each penny to one of the small red hearts.
2. Place the large heart on the floor with the chair beside it. Draw one black dot in the center of the heart.
3. Have the first player step up on the chair with the three heart-pennies.
4. Drop the heart-pennies from above to the heart below. Try to drop the heart-penny on the dot in the center of the heart. If the player's heart-penny lands on the dot, he gets a prize. Give each player at least one turn.

MATCH THE "POSTMARKS"

MATERIALS YOU WILL NEED

six 3"x5" cards per player.
three matching sets of stickers or
designs for each player

WHAT TO DO

1. Discuss what a postmark is, and show the children what one looks like on an envelope.
2. Place one sticker on each card, making one matching set of cards.
3. Give each child one of the cards in the set, then hide the matching cards in a given area.
4. Have the children find the matching "Postmark" around the room.
5. Older children can design their own postmarks then copy the match to make the set.

Variation: Play Concentration or Memory Games with the cards turned upside down. Have the children playing find pairs.

VALENTINE WORD LIST

Look over this list of Valentine words, then choose an activity below which will be appropriate for your children.

POLITENESS:	RIGHTS:
SHARING:	RESPECT:
PEACE:	PRIVILEGE:
FREEDOM:	EQUALITY:
FRIENDSHIP:	INDIVIDUALISM:
AGREEMENT:	HONOR:
CHARITABLE:	SELF:
NEIGHBORLY:	LOVE:
BROTHERHOOD:	FAIR:
HOPE:	GENEROSITY:

- ACTIVITY 1: Discuss the definition of these words with the children.

- ACTIVITY 2: Write each of the words above on a 3"x5" card. Mix them up and hand them out. Have a group or a child act out the meaning of the word on each card. The rest of the group must guess the word.

- ACTIVITY 3: Give each child a list of the words in one column, and the definitions in another. Match the definitions with the words.

- ACTIVITY 4: Have each child or a small group of children give their own definition of the words (or word).

- ACTIVITY 5: Have each child write what our world would be like if none of the above words, thoughts, or deeds existed.

- ACTIVITY 6: Have the children discuss, or illustrate, why we need to live these concepts every day in order to get along with our fellow man.

- ACTIVITY 7: Write a story about how you incorporated one of these values in your life.

AIRBORNE MESSAGE OF GOOD WILL

MATERIALS YOU WILL NEED

helium balloon
small postcard
pencil
fine string or heavy thread
scissors

WHAT TO DO

1. Write a pleasant note on only the top half of the post card. Leave space for the receiver to respond. Address the postcard to your school (not you!!) and stamp it.
2. Punch a hole in the corner and tie the string through it. Tie the other end of the string to the balloon.
3. Go outside and let the balloon go! Watch the mailbox for an answer.

THE BILLY GOATS' VALENTINE

(a wiggle-with-me story)

by Susan Olson Higgins

Instructions: All children should stand quietly in a space where they can wiggle without bumping each other.

When they hear this word: **the action is:**

jump	jump, jump, jump
one	clap
three	clap, clap, clap
brook	"gurgle, gurgle, gurgle"
clomp	stomp, stomp, stomp
munch	chew, chew, chew
quiet	"sh-h-h-h"
peaceful	"ho-hum"
hopped	hop, hop, hop

Once upon a time there were three *(clap, clap, clap)* billy goats. They lived on a hill not far from a gurgling brook *(gurgle, gurgle, gurgle)*. Every morning they would clomp *(stomp, stomp, stomp)* over the bridge. They would munch *(chew, chew, chew)* green grass, and drink at the gurgling brook *(gurgle, gurgle, gurgle)*. They led a quiet *(sh-h-h-h)*, peaceful *(ho-hum)* life.

One day the three *(clap, clap, clap)* billy goats clomped *(stomp, stomp, stomp)* over the bridge to munch *(chew, chew, chew)* green grass and drink at the gurgling brook *(gurgle, gurgle, gurgle)*. As they clomped *(stomp, stomp, stomp)* along, they noticed that something was v-e-r-y different. The three *(clap, clap, clap)* billy goats looked to the left and to the right and alllll around them to see how their quiet *(sh-h-h-h)*, peaceful *(ho-hum)* hillside had changed.

Suddenly, one of the three *(clap, clap, clap)* billy goats shouted, "Look! Everything has turned red!" It was true. The three *(clap, clap, clap)* billy goats' quiet *(sh-h-h-h)*, peaceful *(ho-hum)* world was rosy and pink and red! The three *(clap, clap, clap)* billy goats were soooooo surprised that they jumped! *(jump, jump, jump)*.

They began to run helter skelter over the hillside. One *(clap)* billy goat clomped *(stomp, stomp, stomp)* over the bridge. One *(clap)* billy goat jumped *(jump, jump, jump)* through the bushes. And one *(clap)* billy goat hopped *(hop, hop, hop)* to the garden searching for answers. They wondered why their hillside was red!

Then a tiny butterfly floated by, leaving a trail of red wherever it flew. It flitted up and over, around and under every bush, tree, flower, and blade of grass. As it flew, everything turned red. The three *(clap, clap, clap)* billy goats were amazed. "Why are you painting everything red?" they asked.

The butterfly flew over to them and gently landed on the tail of one *(clap)* of the billy goats. "Don't you know what day this is?" asked the butterfly? "No!" answered the three *(clap, clap, clap)* billy goats. "Why, today is Valentine's Day!" answered the butterfly as it spread its beautiful wings and flew off to continue painting the hillside red.

The three *(clap, clap, clap)* billy goats jumped *(jump, jump, jump)* in the air and clomped *(stomp, stomp, stomp)* over the bridge. They hopped *(hop, hop, hop)* through the red flowers where they came together nose to nose over the tulips. They rubbed noses, which is "I am sooo glad you are my friend," in billy goat. Then they had, a very happy, quiet *(sh-h-h-h)*, peaceful *(ho-hum)*, Valentine's Day, munching *(chew, chew, chew)* the delicious Valentine grass, and drinking the sweet water from the gurgling brook *(gurgle, gurgle, gurgle)* . . . . .

. . . until THE END of Valentine's Day!

55

Delectable
Delicious
and
Dainty
Treats

LOVE JUICE

INGREDIENTS YOU WILL NEED

one can frozen fruit punch   punch bowl
water   spoon
strawberry sherbet   cups
7-Up

WHAT TO DO

1. Mix the fruit punch according to directions.
2. Add fruit punch to 7-Up in punch bowl.
3. Add sherbet to taste. (Just enough to float on the top should suffice.)
4. Serve in paper cups.

CINDY'S HEART SHAPED SHORT BREAD RECIPE

INGREDIENTS YOU WILL NEED

3/4 lb. butter softened (or 3 cubes)
1 cup sugar
3 cups pre-sifted flour
granulated sugar in a small bowl
extra flour
cutting board
heart-shaped cookie cutters
bowl
spoons
oven
rolling pin
refrigerator
cookie sheet
an adult to supervise

WHAT TO DO

1. Cream sugar and butter together.
2. Work in flour.
3. Chill for 1-2 hours.
4. Roll out on lightly floured cloth covered cutting board.
5. Roll to 1/2" thick.
6. Cut into heart shapes using cookie cutters.
7. Sprinkle tops with granulated sugar.
8. Place onto ungreased cookie sheet.
9. Bake at 350 degrees for 20 minutes OR until the edges are just starting to brown.
10. M-m-m-m! They get better with age if stored over night in a cookie tin!

OLD-OLD FASHIONED VALENTINE QUICK CAKE

INGREDIENTS YOU WILL NEED

2 eggs
cream
1 cup sugar
1 cup flour
1 teaspoon baking powder
2 layer cake pans (heart-shaped preferred)
flour and grease for sides and bottom of pans
whipped cream
strawberries ... frozen or fresh
bowls
spoons
spatula
hot pads
oven
an adult to supervise

WHAT TO DO

1. Break eggs into a cup.
2. Fill the rest of the cup with sweet cream.
3. Beat well and add sugar as you beat.
4. Add flour and baking powder.
5. Pour equal amounts into 2 greased and floured cake pans.
6. Bake in a moderate oven, about 350 degrees for 20-30 minutes, checking the center to see if it is done. If it bounds back to touch, it is done.
7. Use whipped cream for center filling and top.
8. Add "heart-shaped" strawberries for a topping.
9. Delicious!

58

AURELIA'S CHOCOLATE HEART SWIRLS

INGREDIENTS YOU WILL NEED

pre-baked heart-shaped sugar cookies
sauce pan
spoon
spatula
pastry bag
chocolate chip morsels
stove top or hot plate
an adult to supervise

WHAT TO DO

1. Melt the chocolate chip morsels over a **low** heat in the sauce pan.
2. Drip the melted chocolate into the pastry bag.
3. Allow the children to taken turns squeezing chocolate designs onto the heart-shaped sugar cookies.

CUPID'S SANDWICH

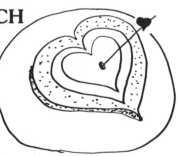

INGREDIENTS YOU WILL NEED

ham slices
cheese slices
bread
butter
olives
toothpicks with paper hearts on the end
heart-shaped cookie cutter
bread and butter knife
an adult to supervise

WHAT TO DO

1. Cut the ham and cheese slices into hearts with the cookie cutter.
2. Cut the bread into heart shapes with the cookie cutters. Butter each side
3. Place the ham and cheese on the bread with an olive on top. Hold it in place with a toothpick.
4. Serve to Cupid and friends!

BILLY GOATS' VALENTINE COOKIES

(Bake these after reading the "The Billy Goats' Valentine," an action story on page 54.)

INGREDIENTS YOU WILL NEED

2 eggs
1 cup brown sugar
1/2 cup melted butter
1/2 teaspoon soda
1-1/2 cups flour
1 teaspoon cinnamon
pinch of salt
1/2 lb. dates
1/4 lb. nutmeats
greased cookie pan
spoons
spatula
bowl
oven
an adult to supervise

WHAT TO DO

1. Beat eggs. Add brown sugar and melted butter.
2. Add soda dissolved in a tiny bit of hot water.
3. Add flour sifted with cinnamon and salt.
4. Add dates and nutmeats.
5. Drop by spoon on a greased cookie sheet.
6. Bake at 350 degrees for 8-12 minutes, or until done.

m-m-m-m ICE CREAM
WITH PEPPERMINT STICK SAUCE

INGREDIENTS YOU WILL NEED

ice cream
1 cup sugar
2/3 cup white syrup
1/3 cup water
candy thermometer
1 cup evaporated milk
cold water
3/4 cup finely ground peppermint stick candy
spoon
sauce pan
serving bowls
stove top or hot plate
an adult to supervise

WHAT TO DO

1. Boil 1 cup of sugar, 2/3 cups of white syrup, and 1/3 cup of water together until it forms a firm ball when dropped into cold water (240°F).
2. Slowly stir in 1 cup evaporated milk and 3/4 cup finely-ground peppermint stick candy.
3. Heat over flame until candy is dissolved Do not boil.
4. Spoon over ice cream. Makes 2-1/4 cups, serves 10-12.
5. Serve with a heart-shaped cookie!!

POSTMAN'S GINGERSNAPS

INGREDIENTS YOU WILL NEED

3/4 cup margarine
1 cup brown sugar
1 egg
1/4 cup molasses
2-1/4 cup flour
2 teaspoon baking soda
1 teaspoon cinnamon
1 teaspoon cloves
1/4 teaspoon salt
1 cup chopped nuts
red decorator sugar granules
greased cookie pan
oven
bowls
spoons
spatula
an adult to supervise

WHAT TO DO

1. Mix thoroughly the shortening, brown sugar, egg, and molasses.
2. Blend in the remaining ingredients.
3. Shape dough into balls about the size of a walnut.
4. Dip the tops in red decorator sugar granules.
5. Bake on greased cookie sheet for 10-12 minutes at 375 degrees.
6. Makes about 4 dozen.

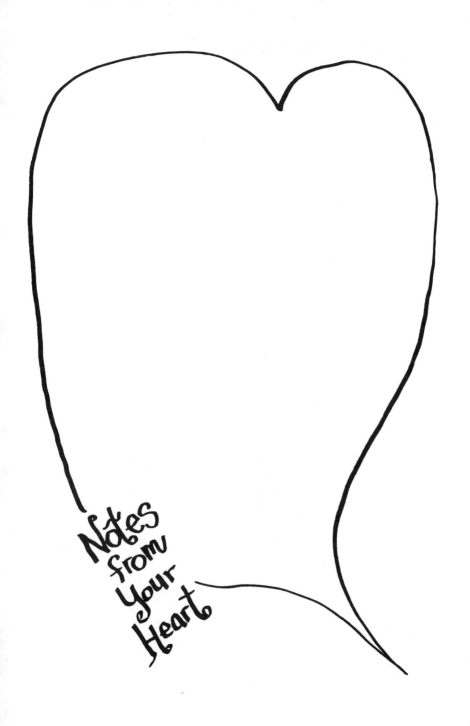

ACKNOWLEDGMENTS

A heartfelt thank you to each of you for sharing your ideas, support, suggestions and your time.

Daniel J. Higgins
Peter Michael Olson Higgins
Joshua Daniel Olson Higgins
Jane Williams
E. Paul Williams
Linda J. Jones
Susan Lynch
Florence Higgins
V.I. Wexner
Joyce Huber
Educational Co-operative School
Shasta Educational Association
Karen Poellet
Dan and Jean Hatch
Cindy Moore
Aurelia Fort
Linda Nelson
Andrea Nelson
Edith Hughes
Mary Burns
Gillian and Charlie Trumbull
Redding Area Co-operative Enrichment Group
Cathy Mayer
Grant Elementary School
Ray Van Diest
Doris Klein
Melvin Phelps
Quinby's of Redding
Donna Majors